My Nursery Book

Illustrated by Penny Ives
Poems chosen by Jenny Wood

DERRYDALE BOOKS
New York

This 1990 edition published by DERRYDALE BOOKS,
distributed by Outlet Book Company, Inc., a Random House
Company, 225 Park Avenue South, New York, New York 10003.

Printed and bound in Italy

ISBN 0–517–053993

8 7 6 5 4 3 2 1

Acknowledgements

The editor and publishers would like to thank the following
for their kind permission to reproduce copyright material
in this book:

Blackie & Son Ltd, Glasgow and London, and Macmillan of
Canada, a division of Canada Publishing Corporation for
"Rock Me Easy", "Silverly" and "Good Night, Good Night"
all by Dennis Lee and all from *Jelly Belly*, copyright 1983 by
Dennis Lee; The author for "My Teddy Bear" and "Sleeping
Outdoors" from *Rhymes About Us*, copyright 1974 by Marchette
Chute; Dutton Children's Books, a division of Penguin Books
USA Inc. for "Jump or Jiggle" by Evelyn Beyer from *Another Here
And Now Story Book* by Lucy Sprague Mitchell, copyright 1937
by E.P. Dutton, renewed 1965 by Lucy Sprague Mitchell; The
author for "After a Bath" by Aileen Fisher; David Higham
Associates Ltd for "There are Big Waves" by Eleanor Farjeon,
from *Then There Were Three* published by Michael Joseph, and
"Caterpillar Walk" and "The Engine Driver" by Clive Sansom
from *The Golden Unicorn* published by Methuen; Margaret Hillert
for "My Teddy Bear" and "Hide-and-Seek-Shadow"; Killian
Jordan for "Mud" by Polly Chase Boyden from "Child Life",
April 1930; Bobbi Katz for "Cat Kisses", reprinted by
permission of Bobbi Katz; James N. Miller for "Shore" by Mary
Britton Miller, copyright Estate of Mary Britton Miller; Spike
Milligan Productions Ltd for "My Sister Laura" by Spike
Milligan; Random Century Limited for "Growing" by Delphine
Evans from *Fingers, Feet and Fun* by Delphine Evans, "In the
Kitchen" and "Come on Board" by Barbara Ireson from *Over
and Over Again* by Barbara Ireson and Christopher Rowe, and
"Hop a Little" by Barbara Ireson and Christopher Rowe from
Over and Over Again by Barbara Ireson and Christopher Rowe;
The Society of Authors as the literary representative of the
Estate of Rose Fyleman for "Singing Time" by Rose Fyleman.

Every effort has been made to trace all the copyright holders
and the Publishers apologize if any inadvertent omission has
been made.

Contents

RISE AND SHINE

Singing Time

I wake in the morning early
And always, the very first thing,
I poke out my head and I sit up
   in bed
And I sing and I sing and I sing.

(Rose Fyleman)

The Cock Does Crow

The cock does crow
To let you know
If you be wise
'Tis time to rise;
For early to bed
And early to rise
Is the way to be healthy
And wealthy and wise.

Cat Kisses

Sandpaper kisses
on a cheek or a chin —
that is the way
for a day to begin!

Sandpaper kisses —
a cuddle, a purr,
I have an alarm clock
that's covered with fur.

(*Bobbi Katz*)

What Shall We Do with a Lazy Katie?

What shall we do with a lazy Katie?
What shall we do with a lazy Katie?
What shall we do with a lazy Katie?
Early in the morning?

Roll her on the bed and tickle her all over,
Roll her on the bed and tickle her all over,
Roll her on the bed and tickle her all over,
Early in the morning.

Heave ho and UP she rises,
Heave ho and UP she rises,
Heave ho and UP she rises,
Early in the morning.

In the Kitchen

The saucepan lids went clang
And the door blew shut with
  a bang,
The kitchen tap went
   shhshhshhshhshh
And the whistling kettle sang.

The timer went off with a ping
And the doorbell began to ring,
The dog joined in with a woof,
  woof, woof,
And then Daddy began to sing!

(Barbara Ireson)

There Was a King

There was a king who had
    four sons,
For breakfast they had
    currant buns,
It seems a funny thing to me,
But every day they each ate
    three.
Every day the baker came,
Every day it was the same,
Every day at half past eight
He left twelve buns at the
    castle gate.

FUN AND GAMES
Counting Rhymes

One, Two, Buckle My Shoe

One, two,
Buckle my shoe;
Three, four,
Open the door;
Five, six,
Pick up sticks;
Seven, eight,
Lay them straight;
Nine, ten,
A big fat hen;

Eleven, twelve,
Dig and delve;
Thirteen, fourteen,
Maids a-courting;
Fifteen, sixteen,
Maids in the kitchen;
Seventeen, eighteen,
Maids in waiting;
Nineteen, twenty,
My plate's empty.

Five Little Monkeys

Five little monkeys walked
along the shore

One got stuck in it, then
there were two.

One went a-sailing, then
there were four.

Two little monkeys found
a currant bun.

Four little monkeys
climbed up a tree

One ran away with it, then
there was one.

One tumbled down, then
there were three.

One little monkey cried all
afternoon

Three little monkeys found
a pot of glue

So they put him in an
aeroplane
And sent him to the moon!

Come on Board

One is one
and two is two,
I'm a spaceman.
Who are you?

Three is three
and four is four,
Listen to my
spaceship's roar.

Five is five
and six is six,
Come on board,
we must be quick!

Seven is seven,
eight is eight,
Wouldn't you like
to be my mate?

Nine is nine
and ten is ten,
You will not see
earth again.

(Barbara Ireson)

Action Rhymes

Round and Round the Garden

Round and round the garden
Like a teddy bear;
One step, two step,
Tickle you under there!

This Little Pig

This little pig went to market,
This little pig stayed at home,
This little pig had roast beef,
This little pig had none,
And this little pig cried:
''Wee, wee, wee, wee, wee, wee,''
All the way home!

Hickory, Dickory, Dock

Hickory, dickory, dock
The mouse ran up the clock.
The clock struck one,
The mouse ran down,
Hickory, dickory, dock.

To Market, To Market

To market, to market,
To buy a fat pig;
Home again, home again,
Jiggety-jig.

To market, to market,
To buy a fat hog;
Home again, home again,
Jiggety-jog.

To market, to market,
To buy a plum bun;
Home again, home again,
Market is done.

19

I'm a Little Teapot

I'm a little teapot, short and
  stout;
Here's my handle,
Here's my spout.
When I see the teacups, hear me
  shout,
"Tip me up and pour me out."

Can You Walk on Tiptoe?

Can you walk on tiptoe,
As softly as a cat?
And can you stamp along
  the road,
Stamp, stamp, just like
  that?

Can you take some great
  big strides,
Like a giant can?
Or walk along so slowly,
Like a poor, bent old man?

An Elephant

An elephant goes like
  this and that.
He's terribly big,
And he's terribly fat.
He has no fingers,
And he has no toes,
But goodness gracious,
  what a nose!

Jelly on the Plate

Jelly on the plate,
Jelly on the plate,
Wibble wobble,
Wibble wobble,
Jelly on the plate.

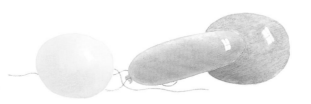

Ten Fingers

I have ten little fingers
And they all belong to me.
I can make them do things.
Would you like to see?

I can shut them up tight
Or open them wide.
I can put them together
Or make them all hide.
I can make them jump high,
I can make them jump low,
I can fold them quietly
And hold them just so.

Growing

See me curl up very small
Like a little tiny ball.
Moving upward very slow
Up and up like people grow.

Now upon my knees I kneel,
I am growing, I can feel.
Moving upwards very slow,
Up and up like people grow.

Now I'm standing straight and
    tall.
I think I'd rather be a ball.
Slowly, slowly to the floor.
Now I'll do it all once more!

(Delphine Evans)

23

Hands Clap

Hands clap,
Fingers wriggle,
Arms wave,
Thumbs wiggle.
Toes waggle,
Heels thump,
Legs run,
Feet jump.

Hop a Little

Hop a little,
Skip a little,
Dance a little,
Then

Jump a little,
Walk a little,
Then begin
Again.

Hop a little,
Skip a little,
Dance a little,
Then

Jump a little,
Walk a little,
Then begin
Again.

(Barbara Ireson and
Christopher Rowe)

25

Singing Rhymes

One Finger, One Thumb, Keep Moving

One finger, one thumb, keep
moving,
One finger, one thumb, keep
moving,
One finger, one thumb, keep
moving,
We'll all be merry and bright.

One finger, one thumb, one arm,
keep moving, etc.

One finger, one thumb, one arm,
one leg, keep moving, etc.

One finger, one thumb, one arm,
one leg, one nod of the head,
keep moving, etc.

One finger, one thumb, one arm,
one leg, one nod of the head,
stand up, sit down, etc.

One finger, one thumb, one arm,
one leg, one nod of the head,
stand up, sit down, turn
around, keep moving, etc.

The Bear Went Over the Mountain

The bear went over the
  mountain,
The bear went over the
  mountain,
The bear went over the
  mountain,
To see what he could see.

And all that he could see,
And all that he could see,
Was the other side of the
  mountain,
The other side of the mountain
The other side of the mountain
Was all that he could see.

The Music Man

I am a music man,
I come from far away,
And I can play —
What can you play?

1   I play pi-a-no,
   Pi-a, pi-a, pi-a-no,
   Pi-a-no, pi-a-no,
   Pi-a, pi-a, pi-a-no.

2   I play the big drum.
   Boom-di, boom-di,
     boom-di-boom,
   Boom-di-boom,
     boom-di-boom,
   Boom-di, boom-di,
     boom-di-boom
   Pi-a, pi-a, pi-a-no,
   Pi-a-no, pi-a-no,
   Pi-a, pi-a, pi-a-no.

OUT & ABOUT

Puddles

There are large puddles, small
  puddles,
All made by the rain,
Brown puddles, black puddles,
Puddles in the lane,
Puddles we step over,
Puddles we jump through,
Cold puddles, warm puddles,
Muddy puddles, too.

There are puddles by the
  wayside,
Puddles in the field,
Puddles gaily shining
Like a soldier's glinting shield.
Puddles that go splash,
Puddles that go splosh.
Puddles here so deep
We need a mackintosh.

(J. Stickells)

Mud

Mud is very nice to feel
All squishy-squashy between the
  toes!
I'd rather wade in wiggly mud
Than smell a yellow rose.

Nobody else but the rosebush
  knows
How nice mud feels
Between the toes.

(*Polly Chase Boyden*)

33

A Kite

I often sit and wish that I
Could be a kite up in the sky,
And ride upon the breeze and
  go
Whichever way I chanced to
  blow.

Picnic Day

Sing a song of
picnics,
Bread and butter
spread,
Greenery all
around about,
And cherries
overhead!

(Rachel Field)

Hide-and-Seek Shadow

I walked with my shadow,
I ran with my shadow,
I danced with my shadow, I did.
Then a cloud came over
And the sun went under
And my shadow stopped playing
And hid.

(Margaret Hillert)

Shore

Play on the seashore
And gather up shells,
Kneel in the damp sands
Digging wells.

Run on the rocks
Where the seaweed slips,
Watch the waves
And the beautiful ships.

(Mary Britton Miller)

There are Big Waves

There are big waves and little
  waves,
Green waves and blue,
Waves you can jump over,
Waves you dive through.

Waves that rise up
Like a great water wall,
Waves that swell softly
And don't break at all.

Waves that can whisper,
Waves that can roar,
And tiny waves that run at you
Running on the shore.

(Eleanor Farjeon)

Caterpillar Walk

High on a leaf,
As happy as could be,
There sat a little caterpillar
Nibbling at a tree.

He went for a walk
With his one, two, three,
A fat little caterpillar
Creeping on a tree.

(Clive Sansom)

A Big Turtle

A big turtle sat on
the end of a log,
Watching a tadpole
turn into a frog.

Jump or Jiggle

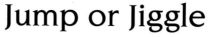

Frogs jump
Caterpillars hump

Worms wiggle
Bugs jiggle

Rabbits hop
Horses clop

Snakes slide
Seagulls glide

Mice creep
Deer leap

Puppies bounce
Kittens pounce

Lions stalk —
But —
I walk!

(Evelyn Beyer)

39

Down at the Station

Down at the station, early in the
  morning,
See the little puffer trains all in
  a row.
See the engine driver pull the
  little handle.
Choo, choo, choo, and off we go.

The Engine Driver

The train goes running along
    the line,
Jicketty-can, jicketty-can.
I wish it were mine, I wish it
    were mine,
Jicketty-can, jicketty-can.
The Engine Driver stands in
    front —
He makes it run, he makes it
    shunt.

Out of the town,
Out of the town,
Over the hill,
Over the down,
Under the bridges,
Across the lea,
Over the ridges,
And down to the sea,

With a jicketty-can, jicketty-can,
Jicketty-jicketty-jicketty can,
Jicketty-can, jicketty-can . . .

(*Clive Sansom*)

41

STORYTIME

Five Little Chickens

Said the first little chicken,
With a weird little squirm,
''I wish I could find
A fat little worm.''

Said the next little chicken,
With an odd little shrug,
''I wish I could find
A fat little slug.''

Said the third little chicken,
With a sharp little squeal,
"I wish I could find
Some nice yellow meal."

Said the fourth little chicken,
With a small sigh of grief,
"I wish I could find
A little green leaf."

Said the fifth little chicken,
With a faint little moan,
"I wish I could find
A wee gravel stone."

"Now, see here," said the
    mother,
From the green garden
    patch,
"If you want your breakfast,
Just come here and scratch."

43

Jeremiah Obadiah

Jeremiah Obadiah, puff, puff,
  puff,
When he gives his messages he
  snuffs, snuffs, snuffs,
When he goes to school by day,
  he roars, roars, roars,
When he goes to bed at night he
  snores, snores, snores.
When he goes to Christmas
  treats he eats plum-duff,
Jeremiah Obadiah, puff, puff,
  puff.

My Sister Laura

My sister Laura's bigger than me
And lifts me up quite easily.
I can't lift her, I've tried and
  tried;
She must have something heavy
  inside.

(*Spike Milligan*)

There Was a Crooked Man

There was a crooked man,
And he walked a crooked mile.
He found a crooked sixpence
Against a crooked stile;
He bought a crooked cat,
Which caught a crooked mouse,
And they all lived together
In a little crooked house.

Miss Polly Had a Dolly

Miss Polly had a dolly
Who was sick, sick, sick.
So she phoned for the doctor
To be quick, quick, quick.
The doctor came
With his bag and his hat,
And he rapped at the door
With a rat-tat-tat.

He looked at the dolly
And he shook his head.
Then he said, "Miss Polly,
Put her straight to bed."
He wrote on a paper
For a pill, pill, pill;
"I'll be back in the morning
with my bill, bill, bill."

I Had a Little Nut Tree

I had a little nut tree,
Nothing would it bear
But a silver nutmeg
And a golden pear;
The King of Spain's daughter
Came to visit me,
And all for the sake
Of my little nut tree.
I skipped over water,
I danced over sea,
And all for the sake
Of my little nut tree.

Hey Diddle Diddle

Hey diddle diddle,
The cat and the fiddle,
The cow jumped over
the moon;
The little dog laughed
To see such sport
And the dish ran away
with the spoon.

Higglety, Pigglety, Pop!

Higglety, pigglety, pop!
The dog has eaten the mop;
The pig's in a hurry,
The cat's in a flurry,
Higglety, pigglety, pop!

Cock-a-Doodle-Doo

Cock-a-doodle doo,
My dame has lost
  her shoe,
My master's lost his
  fiddling stick,
And doesn't know
  what to do!

Fiddle-De-Dee

Fiddle-de-dee, fiddle-de-dee,
The fly shall marry the
  bumblebee.
They went to church, and
  married was she:
The fly has married the
  bumblebee.

49

AND SO TO BED

The Way They Scrub

The way they scrub
Me in the tub,
I think there's
Hardly
Any
Doubt
Sometime they'll rub
And rub and rub
Until they simply
Rub
Me
Out.

(A.B. Ross)

After a Bath

After a bath
I try, try, try
To wipe myself
Till I'm dry, dry, dry.

Hands to wipe
And fingers and
  toes
And two wet legs
And a shiny nose.

Just think how much
Less time I'd take
If I were a dog
And could shake,
  shake, shake.

(Aileen Fisher)

Go to Bed Late

Go to bed late,
Stay very small;
Go to bed early,
Grow very tall.

Wee Willie Winkie

Wee Willie Winkie runs through the town,
Upstairs and downstairs in his nightgown,
Rapping at the window, crying through the lock;
''Are all the children in their beds, it's past eight o'clock?''

Niddledy, Noddledy

Niddledy, noddledy,
To and fro.
Tired and sleepy,
To bed we go.

Jump into bed,
Switch out the light,
Head on the pillow,
Shut your eyes tight.

Diddle, Diddle, Dumpling

Diddle, diddle, dumpling, my
   son John,
Went to bed with his trousers
   on;
One shoe off, and
   one shoe on,
Diddle, diddle,
   dumpling, my
   son John.

Rock Me Easy

Rock me easy,
Rock me slow,
And rock me where
The robins go,

And rock the branch,
And rock the bough,
And rock the baby
Robins now,

And rock them up
And rock them down
And rock them off
To sleepy town,

And rock me slowly
Up the stairs
To snuggle down
With my teddy bears,

And rock me easy,
Rock me slow,
And rock me where
The robins go.

(Dennis Lee)

Teddy Bear, Teddy Bear

Teddy bear, teddy bear,
Go upstairs.
Teddy bear, teddy bear,
Say your prayers.
Teddy bear, teddy bear,
Turn out the light,
Teddy bear, teddy bear
Say good night.

My Teddy Bear

A teddy bear is a faithful friend.
You can pick him up at either
  end.
His fur is the color of breakfast
  toast,
And he's always there when you
  need him most.

(Marchette Chute)

56

My Teddy Bear

A teddy bear is nice to hold.
The one I have is getting old.
His paws are almost wearing out
And so's his funny furry snout
From rubbing on my nose of
  skin,
And all his fur is pretty thin.
A ribbon and a piece of string
Make a sort of necktie thing.
His eyes came out and now
  instead
He has some new ones made
  of thread.
I take him everywhere I go
And tell him all the things I
  know.
I like the way he feels at night,
All snuggled up against me tight.

(*Margaret Hillert*)

57

Star Light, Star Bright

Star light, star bright.
First star I see tonight.
I wish I may, I wish I might,
Have the wish I wish tonight.

Silverly

Silverly, silverly,
Over the trees
The moon drifts
By on a runaway breeze.

Dozily, dozily,
Deep in her bed,
A little girl
Dreams with the
Moon in her head.

(Dennis Lee)

Twinkle, Twinkle, Little Star

Twinkle, twinkle, little star,
How I wonder what you are.
Up above the world so high,
Like a diamond in the sky.

Sleeping Outdoors

Under the dark
is a star,
Under the star
is a tree,
Under the tree
is a blanket,
And under the
blanket is me.

(Marchette Chute)

59

Good Night, Good Night

The dark is dreaming.
Day is done.
Good night, good night,
To everyone.

Good night to the birds,
And the fish in the sea,
Good night to the bears
And good night to me.

(Dennis Lee)

61